The Natural Rights Conservatism of Rush Limbaugh:

The National Sovereignty/Populist Foundation of a New Entrepreneurial Capitalist Economy.

Laurie Thomas Vass

Copyright © 2021

I0135218

The Great American Business & Economics Press.
GABBYPress.

The Great American Business & Economics Press
GABBY Press

ISBN: 978-1-5136-8335-5

Table of Contents

The Natural Rights Conservatism of Rush Limbaugh:

Chapter 1. Is It Time to Panic?

Beginning in the fall of 2008, just prior to Obama's election, listeners to the Rush Limbaugh program would call in, and frantically ask Rush if it was time to panic.

Rush would always tell them, in a very soothing, reassuring voice, that it was not time to panic, and he assured his listeners that he would tell them when it is was time to panic.

We begin by reviewing the transcripts of these calls to explain that the response that Rush gave to his listeners provides insight into establishing his natural law and natural rights philosophy.

One of our missions is to piece together a coherent, comprehensive political philosophy of Rush's opinions by examining his statements on the issues over a 30-year history of broadcasting.

Another part of our mission is to counter-attack the sordid, sleazy intellectual work of Marxist Democrats about Rush's natural rights philosophy, after his death.

A third part of our mission is to place our interpretation of Rush's natural law/natural rights philosophy into the constitutional framework of a democratic republic, whose end goal is the defense of liberty in an entrepreneurial capitalist economy.

Before we begin, it is fair, as Jefferson noted in the Declaration, that a decent respect for the opinions of mankind requires that I establish my credentials to place his statements into a larger natural rights ideological framework.

I sent this rendition of my early experience listening to Rush's program to his website before he died.

I began listening to Rush in the Fall of 1988, on WPTF, in Raleigh, North Carolina. At first, I was bewildered by what I was hearing, and became more bewildered during my 6 hour Fall trips to Hatteras to fish for gigantic Blues and Stripers.

Our family tradition was to leave Raleigh around midnight, in order to make it to Hatteras by 6 am, at sunrise. At that time, WPTF would play Rush live, during the day, and then put him on a taped program again at midnight.

We would listen to Rush, as we left Raleigh, and the WPTF signal soon became intermixed with a station that was carrying George Noury's program Coast to Coast AM.

As we made our way down to Wilson, N. C., on U. S. 64, we would hear snippets of Rush, talking about Reagan, and the Democrats, intermingled with Noury, talking about aliens.

For the longest time, in October of 1988, we thought that Rush Limbaugh and George Noury may be the same person, or perhaps two people on the same program.

Our family tradition was to stop at the top of Bonner Bridge, over the Oregon Inlet, usually around 4 am, to sing and dance, and revel in the joy of arriving at Hatteras.

In those first couple of trips, at the top of Bonner Bridge, I remember asking the others, "What the Hell was that we were listening to?"

It took me several months to appreciate what Rush was doing, and I never stopped listening to him for the next 31 years.

My credentials for writing this article are based upon 31 years of being a fan of Rush Limbaugh.

Callers into the Rush Limbaugh radio program were expressing a common despair about why the Republicans, in 2008, did not fight to protect individual freedoms from Obama's socialist transformation of America, when the moment of battle with global socialist tyranny arrived.

Limbaugh's response to the callers went through a transformation, primarily from being a defender of Bush, and the status quo Republicans, to being more like the arguments of the anti-federalists in 1787, against Madison's centralized government.

His explanation of the failure for the Republicans to respond to Obama's threat to liberty was that the Republicans were a part of "the political elite in Washington."

Beginning in October, 2008, the first caller to use the phrase "time to panic" stated:

> Oct 3, 2008 Folks, It's Not Time to Panic? Yet
>
> RUSH: Bill in New Castle, Pennsylvania, welcome to the EIB Network, sir. Hello.
>
> CALLER: — that you're going to tell me when to start panicking, but I'm panicking now.

RUSH: Don't. Don't any of you people start panicking, now. Fear can be a good motivator, but panic isn't. You've gotta stay involved out there. You cannot get so dispirited that you think it's pointless to show up and vote on Election Day.

From that first call in 2008, callers repeatedly asked Rush if it was time to panic.

Oct 16, 2008 If Obama Wins (and It's Not Over), America Faces Dire Consequences

CALLER: Like you said, it's not time for us to panic. (laughing)

RUSH: I'll tell you when it's time to panic. Obama I think wants this for totally different reasons than McCain does. Obama wants this to reshape America. He really wants this to reshape what this country is. McCain's motivation for this is — I'm not saying he doesn't have a great motivation, but he doesn't think this way, he doesn't think in terms of ideology, he doesn't think in terms of socialist, capitalist, and so forth. He just doesn't. So this is why I've been saying we're going to have to drag him across the finish line. I don't mean to be insulting in that way but somebody's going to have to spell out, like we all are doing, what we face if he loses.

Jan 31, 2013. No, It's Not Time to Panic.

RUSH: Here's Joe in St. Louis. Joe, thanks for the call. You're up next.

RUSH: It's not time to panic yet. People continue to ask the question. I can't tell you specifically — and you know, I'm not into false hope, and I don't lie to myself. I just have… I don't know, folks, I just can't believe we're gonna lose this country. And I don't believe we have.

Oct 12, 2016 No, It's Still Not Time to Panic Yet

RUSH: Here's Margot in Charles City, Iowa. Welcome to the program, Margot. Great to have you here.

CALLER: I am in panic mode. You said don't panic until you tell us when to panic. And last night my husband and I watched Hillary's America movie, which I could not find in a theater anywhere, so I advanced ordered a DVD. We sat down together and watched it last night, and, Rush, I am a longtime conservative, 64-year-old Catholic woman. I am scared to death. I don't sleep. I'm an absolute basket case, and I want what's good for my children, my grandchildren, my family. It's all going down the tubes because, after watching that movie last night, all I saw was what's coming down, what's next, what they have planned —

The caller below is representative of this expression of despair about why the Republicans were failing to fight against the socialists, with Limbaugh's explanation that Republicans were scared of being called racists by the Democrats.

April 26, 2011. BEGIN TRANSCRIPT.

CALLER: I want to tell you up front I'm on a cell phone, so we have that out of the way. But I wanted to try to explain why I think that Donald Trump, who I think is just a horrible candidate for the Republicans, is catching on with so many Republicans. It's because he talks like he's got some balls. And

I'm begging, I'm begging for
somebody in the Republican Party to
step forward that's got some balls.
You know what I'm saying?

RUSH: I do think he [Trump]   has a
skewed view of conservatism. I
do. I think   somebody's given him a
bit of a misread on the conservative
base. So I'll grant   you that. But it
is a problem. Look, I'm not being
serious. I was joking. I know what you
mean when you say people lack
some fortitude. I don't know what
the fear is. I mean I've tried to figure
it out. I've considered still a fear of
race, any criticism of Obama is gonna
result in being called racist. That
fear I think is always gonna be there.
I think fear of the   Republican
hierarchy. There is this notion that
you wait 'til it's your turn.

Over a period of several years, Limbaugh's
explanation of the Republican behavior began to
change to incorporate a type of political
symbiosis between the Republicans and the
Democrats.

He began to explain that all special interests
tended to form a coalition in Washington, that he
calls the "political elite."

June 14, 2013. BEGIN
TRANSCRIPT.

RUSH: Kansas City. Betty, hi.
Welcome to the EIB Network. Great to
have you here. Hello.

CALLER: Hi, Rush. I was reading
the   website, and I think that
someone said this yesterday, but
I was driving down the road, and
you were saying we're just
missing something on the amnesty
bill, why in the world would
Republicans support something
that   will cause their party to lose
in the future. And I was just thinking,
well, they'll just   become the
Democrats -- now, I'm probably
being reactionary, but   I'm
thinking, they'll probably just
become the Democrats that they are
already are. I am so disappointed in
my party. I expect to disagree with
the Democrat Party. But I disagree
with my party. I'm a Republican, or at
least I thought I was.

RUSH: The bottom line is that the
Republican Party is embarrassed by its
own base. The Republican Party is
ashamed of its base. They accept the

Democrat caricature of the Republican
base. Southern, hayseed hicks, pro-
lifers, pickup-truck-driving, gun-rack-
in-the-back-window people,
chewing tobacco and going to church
and talking about God all the time.

But they really see 'em as a bunch of
zealots when it comes to abortion.
And all these guys I'm talking about
have wives who nag 'em about it,
don't want any part of the pro-life
crowd, embarrassed to be with them
at the conventions. So the theory goes
that this is a way to get   rid of the
Republican base. Supporting
amnesty and having the   Democrats
win big-time elections after this is a
way for the party to finally get rid of
its base. Now, you say, "Well,
replace it with what?"

In the most recent period, Limbaugh sharpened
his criticism of the Republican Party to include an
explanation of why Republicans cooperate with
Democrats, when cooperation could possibly
result in the death of the Republican Party.

January 14, 2014. BEGIN
TRANSCRIPT.

RUSH: Look at every issue that
comes up. They give the Democrats all
or a part of what they want trying to buy
peace and love and affection, and it just
never works. So extending
unemployment benefits... Here's
Obama's economic policy: Extending
federal unemployment benefits,
raising the federal minimum wage, and
amnesty. That's Obama's big economic
push. That's what we're told is going
to be his focus in the State of the
Union show.

January 24, 2014. BEGIN
TRANSCRIPT.

RUSH: So, I mean, the upshot here is
that you take a look at any national
poll, immigration reform, amnesty,
it's nowhere near the top when people
are asked to name the most
important issues they think are facing
the country. No reason to do this. And
yet the Republican leadership is as
desirous and as action oriented, if not
more so, than the Democrat majority
is in pushing for amnesty. Yet it's the
law of the land. But the House

Republican leadership wants to go
for it.

Now, we know why. Chamber of
Commerce and moneyed donors.
Donors to mainstream Republicans are
saying they want amnesty, they need the
new cheap labor, they can't keep
going like this. They need it and
they'll do anything they can to get it. If it
takes amnesty, fine. They don't care
about the cultural impact or the rest of it;
they just need the labor. And these
people depend on these donors for
reelection, and so that explains it. Yet
it's the law of the land.

By 2014, Limbaugh was becoming increasingly
skeptical about the principles that guided the
Republican Party.

January 31, 2014. BEGIN
TRANSCRIPT.

RUSH: Now, let me close the loop
on immigration. We sit here, it
doesn't make any sense. It's the end
of the Republican Party. The
polling data all shows it. The people
that would be granted amnesty are
not gonna vote Republican because
of this or anything else. I mean, not

without a lot of work. And the
Republican Party being so
publicly for amnesty is not going to
change how these people vote. I
don't know if the Republicans think
that's going to happen. I do know
that the prevailing thought or theory
is really baked in total
defensiveness.

Why are the Republicans willing to
commit suicide? Because that's what it is.

The fact is we haven't seen the
Republican Party act much like the
opposition party yet. Whenever some
individual   Republicans do pop
up in opposition, they get cut down
by other Republicans. I'm gonna
tell you,folks, sometimes I end up
angrier at Republicans and what
they're saying than I get at Democrats
these days.

Limbaugh's most recent explanations are getting
closer to the truth about the Republican Party. In
his most recent analysis, Rush was stating that the
Republicans are the party of corporate globalism.

Antipathy toward corporate globalism, or what
Angelo Codevilla describes as the ruling class, is

a primary component in piecing together Rush's natural rights ideology.

It was a mistake for the callers to Rush Limbaugh's program to believe that the Republicans were anything other than the incarnation of the natural aristocracy, under Madison's flawed system of checks and balances.

Those callers just assumed that Republicans would defend liberty because the U. S. Constitution had safeguards that would protect freedom when the battle with socialist tyranny arrived.

The callers discovered that the Republicans have abdicated their historic responsibility to defend constitutional natural rights, because Madison's arrangement did not require that of the Republicans.

The Republicans do not see themselves as the opposition party to the socialists because the socialist agenda of global socialism is not detrimental to the Republican end game of advocating global crony corporatism.

For Republicans, a "more perfect union" means promoting a single special interest of corporate globalism, protected and enhanced by the Federal government.

For Republicans, corporate globalism, and Rush's defense of natural rights, do not connect.

The promotion of the single Republican special interest meant "bipartisanship" with the Democrat Party's socialist agenda. This compatibility of interests between establishment Republican and left-wing Democrats is the same idea that Limbaugh calls "reaching across the aisle."

> Feb 6, 2008. John McCain to Rush Limbaugh: Calm Down, Reach Across Aisle.

> RUSH: When did the measure of conservatism, when did the measure of success, when did the measure of progress, when did it become reaching out to Democrats? If the Republican Party and the Democrat Party were two nations, Senator McCain is saying, 'I'm going to have no border on my nation, the Republican Party. And if those people in that enemy party want to come in, infiltrate our party, that's great. I'm going to show that I'm the guy that can get it done. I'm going to be the guy to not protect the borders.'

Why is it so   hard? I'm serious. This
one escapes me.Why is it so hard to
understand that what we want is to
defeat those people?

The Republican practice of reaching across the
aisle is one reason why Limbaugh suggests that
there should never be compromise with the
socialists because every compromise means
taking one step closer to the irrevocable
tyrannical socialist state.

Several weeks before he died, but after the
election of November 3, 2020, Rush explained
why he never told his listeners that it was time to
panic.

> Nov 6 2021. "You said that you
> would tell us when it's time to panic."
>
> CALLER: You know? I mean, so if
> the election is stolen, 1 see that
> somebody's going to want to be doing
> something going forward to — I
> don't know. We're gonna have to do
> something. We can't just sit back and
> let our country go to hell in a handbag.
>
> RUSH: All right. Full disclosure. A
> number of people have called today,

and Mr. Snerdley has put them up there. "You said that you would tell us when it's time to panic. You said that you thought the election was over. You said this and you said that," and so let me try to answer all of these challenging questions that you have.

I'm never gonna run away from the United States of America. I may die, but I'm not gonna run away from the United States of America. I'm not gonna give up. I am not gonna tell you to give up. I'm not gonna tell you to walk away. I'm not gonna tell you it's time to panic. You can keep asking if you want, but I'm always gonna tell you no.

There will never be walking away. There will never be abandoning the country — and there sure as hell not gonna be me telling you to. That was always designed as a humorous point, like a rhetorical question. "I'll tell you when it's time to panic," but it's never gonna be.

Rush could never bring himself to admit that the United States, as he knew it, was over, and that the nation had died on November 3, 2020, in a successful coup by the Democrat Marxists.

Our interpretation of why he failed to tell his listeners that it was time to panic is that Rush never stopped believing in the principles of greatness of the Nation.

However, Rush never developed a comprehensive political strategy for dealing with the RINO Republicans who colluded with the Democrat Marxists because Rush had implicit faith that, within the two-party political system, that Republicans were the conservative party.

His strategy amounted to an adaptation of the "Buckley Rule" to vote for the most conservative Republican, no matter if the most conservative candidate was a RINO.

His Buckley Rule strategy was flawed because the two-party political system required that the Republicans act as the opposition party to the Democrats.

Rush was still alive to see that America's constitutional system failed on November 3, 2020.

We explain that Rush did not leave America, America left Rush on November 3, 2020..

We agree with Rush that natural rights conservatives do not walk away from the Declaration's expression of natural law and natural rights.

We advise Rush listeners to walk away from the failed nation state created by the Democrat Marxists after their successful coup.

Chapter 2. Rush's Daily Analysis of Issues.

We begin by acknowledging that the term "conservative" has many connotations and definitions. We place the Limbaugh natural rights philosophy within the tradition of natural rights conservatism that originates in the early writing of Thomas Hobbes and John Locke.

The principles that Rush was trying to "conserve" were the principles of liberty of natural law and natural rights, actualized by Jefferson's Declaration.

We have advocated elsewhere, that Trump voters and Rush listeners make a clean distinction between the principles in the Declaration, and Madison's rules of civil procedure, in his constitution of 1787. (Vass. Laurie Thomas, Reclaiming The Spirit of 1776: Jettisoning Madison's Constitution in Order to Connect the Declaration to a Nation of Independent Producers in an Entrepreneurial Capitalist Economy. www.clpnewsnetwork.com).

In that earlier article, we made the claim that Lincoln's interpretation of the Declaration of Independence is the truthful heritage of American liberty. We argue that the Declaration, and not

Madison's constitution, reveals the true ideological intent of the Founders of 1776.

Lincoln sought moral justification for the Civil War in the Declaration because he realized that Madison's document promoted slavery. Lincoln's dilemma was that he could not justify a war to end slavery on a document that promoted slavery.

In citing the Declaration as the moral justification of the Civil War, Lincoln tirelessly repeated his phrase that self-government must be based on principles of justice and right: "the laws of nature and of nature's God," as Jefferson had stated.

Every time Lincoln invoked the Declaration as justification for the War, he would also repeat his dictum that self-government required that citizens must give their permission for the rules and laws passed by their representatives.

Like Lincoln, then, we believe, today, that Rush listeners and Trump voters must make a clean break with Madison's constitution, in order to erect a new nation on the principles of liberty in the Declaration.

The citizens did not give their permission to the Democrat Marxists to impose Marxist, one-party tyranny on the citizens.

We deploy the content of the text of the Declaration to guide us in the identification of Rush's natural rights ideology.

One of our challenges, in piecing together the natural rights ideology of Rush, is that he primary provided contemporary daily analysis of issues. He did not dwell on the scholarly or academic philosophy of natural rights.

Over 30 years of listening to Rush, I could re-state his opinions, almost verbatim, on the following issues:

- Abortion
- Budget & Economy
- Civil Rights
- Corporations
- Crime
- Drugs
- Education
- Energy & Oil
- Environment
- Families & Children
- Foreign Policy
- Free Trade
- Government Reform
- Gun Control

- Health Care
- Homeland Security
- Immigration
- Infrastructure & Technology
- Jobs and Economic Growth
- Principles & Values
- Social Security
- Tax Reform
- War & Peace
- Welfare & Poverty

I suspect that all Rush listeners could also re-state his positions on each issue.

Our methodology for defining Rush's ideology is to review his statements on the issues, and take from those statements, the relevant ideological parts to piece together his broader natural rights philosophy.

For example, we cite the 2009 commentary by Rush when he stated that he hoped Obama failed, as a president.

We extract from his analysis of that issue to a piece of his natural rights philosophy.

In his February 28, 2009, speech to 2009 Conservative Political Action Conference, Rush stated,

> "I want Obama to fail, because I want America to survive. The Democrats hoped George Bush failed [in Iraq]. So what is so strange about being honest to say that I want Barack Obama to fail if his mission is to restructure and reform this country so that capitalism and individual liberty are not its foundation? Why would I want that to succeed? Let me add a caveat here. The New Castrati, guys who have lost their guts, say, "we can't say we want the President to fail, Mr. Limbaugh, because that's like saying you want the country to fail." It's the opposite. I want the country to survive. I want the country to succeed. I want the country to survive as we have known it, as you and I were raised in it."

We glean from Rush's statement about Obama's Marxism, two nuggets of natural rights principles:

"capitalism and individual liberty are its foundation."

Capitalism is an essential component of Rush's philosophy, but we argue that it is a particular variety of capitalism called entrepreneurial capitalism, as opposed to the existing crony corporate capitalism of today.

Entrepreneurial capitalism fits into Rush's philosophy of allowing the greatest opportunity for individuals to achieve financial success.

We cite another example of an analysis of contemporary issues where we find evidence of the natural rights philosophy of Rush, as it relates to God-given natural rights.

Rush stated in his 1993 book, See, I Told You So,

> "Our Constitution only works in a moral society. The Founding Fathers were Bible-believing Christians. And they were quite adamant in stating that the Constitution would work only in the context of a moral society. "Our Constitution was made for moral and religious people," stated John Adams. George Washington s aid,

"Of all the dispositions and habits that lead to political prosperity, religion and morality are indispensable supports." James Madison agreed: "We have staked the future upon our capacity to sustain ourselves according the Ten Commandments of God. The Constitution would only work, they warned, if the society was girded on a bedrock of solid values and Judeo-Christian principles. "

We take from this statement the essential Jeffersonian natural rights principle, that natural rights are derived from God.

We categorize Rush's statements in the context of natural rights according to his statements on individualism, property rights, and free enterprise.

Rush on Individualism:

Nov 19, 2007. Election Issue #1: America's Future.

This election is going to be about the future of the country and whether it's going to drift more towards socialism or whether we're going

to maintain our capitalist roots,
entrepreneurial spirit, rugged
individualism, it's a seminal, serious
question.

Jan 21, 2008. How Rush Chooses
Candidates.

My brand of conservatism is based
on individual entrepreneurism,
rugged self-individualism, telling
people that they're the ones who
make the country work. I think this is
born out by history and people
respond to it. [First criteria] Limited
government. Get government out
of people's way. Number two, belief
in the system that it's people who
make the country work, not
government. Number three, don't
give me a laundry list of policies
without a philosophical
underpinning that explains the
policies. Number four, don't tell me
that government is the agent of
change and that you are going to
lead the government.. And then,
fifth, after all of those things that
I would define as conservative, which

includes the belief that people can triumph over the obstacles in their lives, that they're not incompetent, they're not incapable, and they're not stupid.

Mar 20, 2009. In Defense of Individualism.

Why is the individual important? If you have to explain why the individual is important in the United States of America, then you have to explain freedom.

I mean are you free because you are a member of a group? Or are you free because you are your own soul, endowed by your creator, God, certain inalienable rights: life, liberty, pursuit of happiness. From where does your freedom come?

the whole concept of individual freedom and liberty was the reason we sought independence from the tyranny of King George

Rugged individualism is self-interest, and self-interest is good. Your self-interest is improving the life that your family lives. You want economic opportunity for them. You want social stability for them. You want a relatively crime-free existence.

Nov 15, 2010. Democrats Poison Our Politics.

Our culture of personal responsibility, our culture of rugged individualism, our entrepreneurial spirit, pursuit of excellence, that culture has been poisoned. We now have people looking to government, not for help, but for their existence. We now have government determining people's outcomes by limitation.

Jul 20, 2011. Populism is Not Conservatism.

I use my own life as sort of a guide, and I use the stories of people I know who have come from nothing, and led by their ambition and their desire, which is 80% of achievement... but everybody has more potential than they even know. Everybody has more ability than they know. Everybody can be better than they are, in any number of ways.

Mar 14, 2012. An Assault on the Symbols of America.

RUSH: This is all part of Obama's disdain for the Constitution. Obama, ladies and gentlemen, looks at the Constitution as "rich white man's law." The Founders, in his view, were rich white guys…Obama wants a constitution where the government is supreme and paramount, not the individual. And so he wants to establish separate laws, depending on which tribe or which race you happen to belong to. The Constitution is a rich white man's law. This is all part of it. It's the core philosophy of "Critical Race Theory,"

Rush on the Principles of Conservatism.

Jan 15, 2008. Rush and Newt on Conservatism.

The one thing that I most took from Ronald Reagan, was that he understood that it's the people who make this country work, not politicians, not elected officials. They get in the way. The thing about Reaganism that's inspiring to me is that he went and told people,'Look, this you can do. We are America, shining city on a hill. Capitalism, the American people engaging in commerce, that's the single greatest agent of change in this country, not what happens in Washington.

Jan 8, 2009. Reestablishing Conservatism 101: Be Who You Are and Be Confident.

It's the country we're talking about, right? It's talking about the things we believe in, the future, for those of you that have kids and grandkids. I've got nieces and nephews, you care about the future, this is what it's all about. I told you before the election, this stuff matters, electionshave consequences. Okay, yeah, we're in a hole. But I'm not going to be on the bus when it goes over the cliff.

Jun 5, 2012. What the Partisan Divide Really Means.

There is no hope for compromise here. All of this talk about compromise is drivel. All of this talk of compromise is a sideshow, it's a distraction, and it is part of the arsenal of weaponry, ammo from the left to defeat us. They have no desire to get along with us. Conservatism is a constant daily intellectual application and pursuit. Liberalism is the most gutless thing you can do. It's easy. Let me read to you the charter of the very Foundation that did this survey, the Pew Foundation. The charter of the Pew Freedom Trust "in 1957 spelled out that Pew intended to 'acquaint the American people' with 'the evils of bureaucracy,' 'the values of a free market,' and 'the paralyzing effects of government controls on the lives and activities of people.' Pew also wanted to 'inform our people of the struggle, persecution, hardship, sacrifice and death by which freedom of the individual was won.'"

Aug 9, 2013. Conservatism is the Only "Outreach" the Republican Party Really Needs.

[Conservatives] have a political message that is timeless and speaks to the heart and mind of everybody who can be made to hear it. And it is the language of the founding of this country. It is rooted in the notion   of creation by God. The natural state of that creation is the yearning to be free, and the understanding that those natural rights of freedom come from our creator, from our God, from your higher power, whatever you want to call it.

Fall 2015.

RUSH: Now, look, Trump did not have any language last night for conservatives per se. He didn't say "I believe in limited government. I believe in constitutional government." He didn't do any of that.

Jan 22, 2016.What They're Saying About Trump and National Review — And What It Means.

But National Review's gotta put down a marker. They are establishing who is and who isn't a conservative, and that's one of their roles. But I don't know, folks. I mean, was Mitt Romney conservative? McCain? Is McCainconservative? (interruption) I know. McCain hated conservatives. Quote from National Review. "Some conservatives have made it their business to make excuses for Trump and duly get pats on the head from him. Count us out. Donald Trump is a menace to American conservatism who would take the work of generations and trample it underfoot in behalf of a populism as heedless and crude as the Donald himself."

Rush on the Ruling Class and the Working Class.

Jan 27, 2010. Inside the Beltway Elitists Blast Conservative Ideologues.

You have elitism on parade. An ideologue for liberty is an ideologue for free society. We agree in the natural rights of man, and an ideologue on the left means promoting one or more forms of tyranny. It's the opposite of promoting liberty.

Feb 26, 2016. The New Populism Isn't New.

The past seven years are the manifestation of the horror and the evil and all the rotten, terrible things that can happen when the people are ignored and abandoned and the political class, for the first official time in people's lives. It openly mocks and makes fun of and disregards the people that elect them.

Dec 24, 2018. Trump's Populism and the Republican Base.

This new liberal order that was created after World War II that led to   the rise of globalism and the United

Nations as a center of globalism and the fact that the United States, because of its unfair size and power, was always going to have to apologize or willingly take second status. But it has now evolved into some globalist enterprise, which last week the United Nations runs a story and says that illegal immigration is a human right and that borders are among the most discriminatory things existing in the human condition today. That borders are too limiting, they are negative and so forth. This is where we're headed.

Chapter 3. Placing Rush's Statements Into the Natural Law and Natural Rights American Tradition.

Natural law begins with the premise that laws about human nature can be discerned by human reason, just like the natural laws of gravity, or biology.

Natural law comes first, in the chronology of the ideology of liberty, and from natural law, the natural rights of individuals are deduced.

From the derivation of natural rights, the constitution is written to protect individual rights of life, liberty, and the pursuit of happiness.

Locke deduced that governments were created to protect and conserve the liberty of individuals to pursue their own self-destiny.

As Locke stated, when humans left the state of nature to form governments, they gave up part of their natural rights in order to secure a stable, consistent set of natural rights, protected by government.

Here in brief are Locke's natural rights principles:

- All human beings are born equal in the natural state of things, in the sense that no one has a natural right to govern another. Equal rights to life, liberty, and property follow.
- In the pre-civil state, these rights are often violated because of the unchecked passions of bad men. [Hobbes] Therefore the most urgent purpose of government is to secure those rights.
- Since no one has the right to rule another by nature without that other's consent, government, which limits one's liberty and property, must be based on the consent of the governed.
- Consent in founding means government is established by a contract among the people. Consent in governing means elected representatives. The alternative to consent is slavery.
- There is a right to revolution if government violates either of these criteria (protection of individual rights and consent).
- To secure these rights, government must rule by law: public rules publicly deliberated on and applied equally.

- Liberty is not unlimited, even in the state of nature. This limit is defined by the law of nature, sometimes called the moral law. The civil law must enforce the law of nature in the state of society.

Locke's natural laws in the American natural rights republic were clearly enunciated by Thomas Paine, in his series of pamphlets, the most well known of which is "Common Sense," first published on January 10, 1776.

One of the most important principles of government, for Paine, was that the unalienable truths, identified by Locke, and later adopted by Jefferson in the Declaration, must be "knowable."

"Knowable" used in this historical context is related to knowable as a truth as derived from the Enlightenment rational school.

Paine wrote that,

> "truth reached through the convictions of open inquiry and examination…universal moral truth, must be knowable."

As Michael Zuckert explains, in The Natural Rights Republic,

> "...the evidentness of the truth is contained within the [Locke's] truths themselves...the truths are not affirmed to be in themselves self-evident, only to be held as such by the Americans...the truths are held as if self evident within the political community dedicated to making them effective. The truths serve as the bedrock or first principles of all political reasoning of the natural rights regime."

When Rush uses the phrase "the American founding," he is arguing that socialists reject the logic of the Enlightenment, and do not reason by logical truths.

The socialists use a philosophy of logic called "moral relativism" which contains no independently objective criteria of truth.

For Paine, the new American government must be built on the truth, moral truth, not on power relationships that existed in the mixed British class system.

For Paine, as for Jefferson, the knowable truth was that God had granted citizens certain inalienable rights, commonly called "natural rights."

The new government, said Paine,

> "is derived solely from a sovereign people...mutually and reciprocally maintained principles of nature in society. Freedom and rights mean a perfect equality of them."

The one duty that falls equally on all persons, in a natural rights republic, wrote Paine, is the duty to defend and honor the principle of equal rights.

Liberty, in the moral sense that Paine used it, has a shared common meaning, as expressed in the Declaration, and in the Articles.

When Rush states that Democrat Marxists do not share common values, as expressed by Jefferson, he is explaining the irreconcilable split in ideology between Democrats and natural rights conservatives.

When Rush describes the all-powerful central government he is saying the same thing that Paine said about Madison and Hamilton's Preamble:

"When Madison and Hamilton say that the central government needs more energy, what they want is energy over the citizens. A more perfect union means a nominal nothing without principles."

When Madison and Hamilton suggested that only the virtuous elite possessed moral values, they denied the moral foundation of Jefferson's natural rights republic that all citizens possessed moral values.

As an example of creating a new government, we cite the work of Thomas Burke, the author of the Nation's first constitution, The Articles of Confederation.

Burke wrote that the new government that aimed to protect individual liberty would consist of these following principles:

- that all sovereign power was in the states separately.
- that the federal government held "expressly" enumerated powers...each state retains its sovereignty, freedom and independence.
- that any right which is not by this confederation "expressly" delegated to the United States in Congress assembled is retained by the states.

- Congress is to be made up of two bodies of delegates, the General Council, and Council of State, with one delegate from each state.
- All bills originate in the General Council, and are read 3 times and passed by a majority in the Council of State.
- Every law must be demonstrated to be within the powers *"expressly delegated to Congress."*

Whenever Rush uses the term "limited central government," he is expressing the ideology of Burke, who created a state sovereignty framework of government.

Burke's term, "expressly delegated," appears over and over again in the debates and resolutions of the Second Continental Congress.

Burke believed that,

> "the authority of the congress rested on the prior acts of the several states, to which the states gave their voluntary consent, and until those obligations were fulfilled, neither nullification of the authority of congress, exercising its due powers, nor secession from the compact

itself was consistent with the terms of their original pledges."

Burke's intent in writing the Articles was "to secure and perpetuate mutual friendship and intercourse among the people of the different States in this union."

Burke wrote,

> "The purpose of the confederation is for the "States hereby severally to enter into a firm league of friendship with each other, for their common defense, the security of their liberties, and their mutual and general welfare, binding themselves to assist each other, against all force offered to, or attacks made upon them, or any of them, on account of religion, sovereignty, trade, or any other pretense whatever."

Burke believed that,

> "the authority of the congress rested on the prior acts of the several states, to which the states gave their voluntary consent, and until those obligations were fulfilled, neither nullification of the authority of congress, exercising its due

powers, nor secession from the compact itself was consistent with the terms of their original pledges."

According to Article XIII of the Confederation, any alteration of the Articles had to be approved unanimously.

Of course, this is the basis of the moral transgression of the unconstitutional act committed by Madison and Hamilton in overthrowing the Articles in 1787.

As Burke wrote,

> "The Articles of this Confederation shall be inviolably observed by every State, and the Union shall be perpetual; nor shall any alteration at any time hereafter be made in any of them; unless such alteration be agreed to in a Congress of the United States, and be afterwards confirmed by the legislatures of every State."

One of the reasons that Madison's constitution ended in the failure of a centralized elite tyranny is that Madison deleted the state's authority to limit the power of the central government in his document of 1787.

Madison knew full well what the legal implications would be, if he allowed the full term, "expressly delegated" to be inserted in the Constitution of 1787 or two years later, in the 9th and 10th amendments in the Bill of Rights.

Madison's deletion of "expressly delegated," created an all-powerful central government, not the limited government advocated by Rush.

The Continental Congress adopted the Articles of Confederation, as amended by Burke, on November 15, 1777.

The first state to ratify the Articles of Confederation was Virginia on December 16, 1777; the thirteenth state to ratify was Maryland, on February 2, 1781.

The ratification of the Articles of Confederation by all 13 states of the new United States Constitution occurred on March 1, 1781.

When Burke began his work on the Articles, in August of 1776, he was working from the principles of liberty drafted by Jefferson, and adopted on July 4, 1776.

According to Jefferson's natural rights philosophy, all human beings possess an original and inherent liberty which is inalienable.

This liberty explains Jefferson, is a liberty for the innocent actions of free citizens, that is, for actions that do not deprive others of their rights, or do not interfere with the realization of the community welfare.

The Declaration is a compact between citizens in each state to establish a rightful centralized political power, dedicated to protecting the natural rights of citizens that are left incompletely protected within each state government.

The Declaration, and the Articles, moved the citizens of the United States toward an egalitarian individualism, with an appeal to natural rights.

Jefferson's natural rights principles were:

- Equality among citizens to participate in government.
- Privacy of citizens from the invasions of agents of government.
- The right to vote in free and fair elections.
- The protection of the natural and property rights of individuals as the supreme goal of government.
- Equal access to the courts and equality before the law.

"No one is born into moral subjugation to political power," stated Jefferson. When citizens leave nature to create their government, "all men are created equal… in nature all humans are equal…not subject to the rightful authority of any other human being…in a state of nature no rightful authority exists in nature. No man is subjected to the will or authority of any other man," he wrote, over and over again, from 1776, to the very last letter he wrote in 1826.

We argue that Jefferson's natural rights principles are the same values shared by Rush, that we gleaned from his above statements on issues.

Chapter 4. Extending Rush's Natural Rights Conservatism.

We argue that Rush's natural rights conservatism can be extended and adapted as the basis of a new constitution, which replaces Madison's flawed class-based document.

That proposed new constitution would restore the original state sovereignty framework of the Articles of Confederation, including Burke's dictum that the Federal government could only act upon authority "expressly delegated" by the states to the Federal government.

As we explain, below, we argue that the new constitution would naturally result in a decentralized entrepreneurial capitalist society.

We further argue, following the work of James Buchanan, formerly of George Mason University, that the social welfare outcomes of that new economy would be superior to the social welfare outcomes of crony capitalism, obtained under the existing constitution.

Locke was a contemporary with David Hume and Francis Bacon in the era of scientific enlightenment, and Locke's contribution was to apply reason to the observation of human nature.

The natural law about humans derived by Locke consisted of two primary human characteristics:

1. Self-preservation and the will to live.
2. Self-improvement and welfare optimization in decision making.

From these two fundamental human characteristics, Locke deduced that governments were created to protect and conserve the liberty of individuals to pursue their own self-destiny, according to natural law.

As Locke stated, when humans left the state of nature to form governments, they gave up part of their natural rights in order to secure a stable, consistent set of natural rights, protected by government.

We note that the second observable natural law, of individual welfare optimization, constitutes the theoretical framework of contemporary neo-classical marginal analysis, which we deploy to argue our case about the superior welfare outcomes of entrepreneurial capitalism.

Locke's two natural laws served as the basis for the instructions that the Continental Congress gave to the states to form their own state constitutions.

Part of our argument about extending Rush's ideology is that those 13 state constitutions were vastly superior to Madison's constitution in protecting natural rights.

On May 10, 1776, the Second Continental Congress adopted John Adams's resolution that,

> " each of the "united colonies adopt such government as shall, in the opinion of the representatives of the people, be best conducive to the happiness and safety of their constituents in particular, and America in general."

Each colony then adopted its own state constitution, and all states, individually, declared their independence from the King.

We note, in passing, that when King George surrendered to the United States, he surrendered to the 13 independent states of America.

The natural rights ideology of the original 13 state constitutions aimed at a type of populist, democratic government of the many, not of the few.

When Madison usurped the authority of the state constitutions, he replaced the government of the many with a government of the few, functioning under the classification of an aristocratic "representative" republic.

As Paine would note, about Madison's 1787 constitution,

> "it is an ill-advised attempt to replicate the British form of mixed constitution...their basis for justice becomes the balancing of particular   class interests....they make it difficult for citizens to   participate...it deprives citizens of private manners and public principles, and is driven by power and not consent, by coercive force and not   the choices of citizens... what they want   is energy over the citizens."

"A more perfect union," said Paine, about Madison's vacuous Preamble,

> "meant a nominal nothing without principles."

In other words, Madison's flawed arrangement unleashed perpetual class warfare in America, exactly as citizens see today with the rhetoric of the race-based, hate mongering Democrat Marxists.

Jefferson wrote that subjugation, coercion, and manipulation arose when the participants to a political or constitutional exchange enter the political relationship with unequal economic power.

In Jefferson's philosophy of natural rights, the force that compels citizen obedience to the constitution is the shared commitment of the right to liberty.

Jefferson wrote that,

> "No one has a right to obstruct another exercising his faculties innocently for the relief of sensibilities made a part of his nature…the right to liberty is an all things equal guarantee of freedom of choice and action…"

Jefferson was addressing the issue Hobbes had raised about the force that would compel obedience to the social order, after the authority of the Pope, and the authority of the King no longer compelled obedience.

When Thomas Hobbes was writing The Leviathan, in the late 1640s, he had two earlier patterns of social authority, the Pope and the

King, to use as examples in developing his own model of civil authority.

Hobbes thought that the primary natural law of humans was the urge to dominate other humans, and he developed this concept of the Leviathan, to compel obedience to the social order.

Jefferson answered Hobbes by stating that the force that creates obedience of the American citizens to obey the constitutional rules in a natural rights republic is the equal opportunity of upward occupational mobility.

As long as every citizen has an opportunity to gain financial success, every citizen supports the equal freedom for any other citizen.

Rush repeated this part of his natural rights ideology, over and over again, during his 31 years of broadcasting.

The extension of Rush's ideology for the new constitution is that upward occupational mobility is the single most important cause of economic growth.

Economic growth leads to a society of "self-made" citizens, who are not dependent on government for welfare.

This connection between the purpose of the constitution and the functioning of the free market is the cause of liberty. The free market entrepreneurial capitalism secures the liberty expressed in the rules of the new constitution.

Madison's constitution created a permanent advantage of unequal economic power for the natural aristocracy over the common citizens. Common citizens entered into Madison's constitutional contract that they had no part in creating or modifying.

The common citizens, in other words, were subjugated, from the start, to the financial interests of the elites. The common citizens endured the conditions of subjugation identified by Jefferson,

> "when the participants to a political or constitutional exchange enter the political relationship with unequal economic power."

Madison's constitution essentially did away with monarchy and the heredity principle but replaced it with power in the hands of an oligarchic class, where the leading families acquired an unbalanced and unchecked political power. (government of the few).

What Madison and Hamilton accomplished in overthrowing Jefferson's natural rights republic, was to re-institute the British class system of unequal economic power, built into the fabric of their constitution of 1787.

Eventually, the elites in the Republican Party assumed this unbalanced political power to use the power of government to direct financial benefits to their own social class, and it is this unchecked power that is so dangerous in the hands of the socialists.

The extension of Rush's natural rights ideology would replace Madison's class and race-based constitution with a constitution whose mission is the defense of liberty, in a democratic republic of the many.

The point is that justice in the natural rights democracy depends on the initial adoption of a unique set of moral values to insure social stability.

Whether this unique constellation of cultural values is widespread and commonly held throughout the society is contingent upon the process of social consensus about the moral values of truth, and fair honest dealings, when citizens leave the state of nature.

The logic of the new natural rights democratic republic, in other words, is that the natural laws of humans provides the rationale for why and how society defines the public purpose of improving individual welfare.

Chapter 5. Placing Rush's Natural Rights Ideology Into The American Populist Tradition.

About 100 years after the adoption and ratification of the Madison's constitution, during one of America's more spectacular economic collapses, the agrarian populist leader, Tom Watson asked in his newspaper, "What is Labor's Fair Share?"

A better question for the agrarian populists may have been

> "What are Fair Constitutional Rules for Labor?"

We cite James Buchanan's, Logical Foundations of Constitutional Liberty. (1999), that any specific configuration of rules in the constitution can lead to diffcrent social welfare outcomes.

For Buchanan, changing the rules on the constitutional input side changes the welfare outcomes in the output side of the economy.

Rush's ideology emphasized fairness in the equal opportunity to achieve success, not in the Democratic Marxist concept of fairness in equal welfare outcomes for all citizens.

The constitutional rules that made life miserable for the farmers in 1887, had been created by Madison and Hamilton, in 1787, to achieve separation of powers in the branches of government, the indirect election of representatives, and judicial review of legislation, all intended to bury any incipient tendencies of a populist citizen's democratic government.

One of the economic outcomes of Madison's stacking the deck in favor of the natural aristocracy was that the greed and corruption of the elites caused a ongoing series of financial collapses, based upon asset speculation, that caused perpetual misery for farmers and the working class.

The populists, of 1887, learned a hard lesson that hard work, by itself, does not insure financial success or lead to upward occupational mobility in America.

Rush never tired of describing the farmers and working classes as the people who do the work, play by the rules, and make the American society prosperous for all citizens.

His natural rights ideology is consistent with Buchanan's concept of constitutional fairness.

The farmers had the right set of values about work and society, but had entered the constitutional contract with unequal economic power.

For the agrarian populists, hard work was associated with the value of independence and the moral value of a person. For farmers, not being dependent on others was the outer sign of moral worth.

In the Savage Ideal, Bruce Clayton notes that in the South,

> "work was a moral absolute, an outer sign of inner worth…"

Rush enjoyed repeating his life story of how he started out, at age 15, working at the bottom of radio broadcasting, and worked his way up the social mobility ladder.

He wanted every citizen who worked hard, like he did, to have the opportunity for success that he had achieved.

Rush wanted citizens to be economically independent, and especially independent of government welfare payments.

This is the same philosophy of fairness and independence expressed by farmers in their populist revolt, in the mid-1880s.

The goal of the farmers was a fair opportunity for financial success, achieved through their labor.

Leonidas Polk, the agrarian leader, who founded N. C. State University, said,

> "Labor is thus associated in our mind with all that is honorable in birth, refined in manners, bright in intellect, manly in character and magnanimous in soul."

The American populist tradition originated in the 10 years prior to the start of the Revolution.

"But, what is a slave?" asked a New Jersey patriot in 1765, "but one who depends upon the will of another for the enjoyment of his life and property."

Dependency, in the minds of farmers, was equated with slavery, and slavery in the American moral setting would be avoided by hard work and fair rules of exchange.

For Rush, dependency on the government is slavery.

No set of policy reforms would ever overcome the flaws of an unbalanced and unfair set of constitutional rules that operated within the social class system built by Madison.

As Charles Beard argued in his 1913 book, An Economic Interpretation of the Constitution of the United States, Madison assumed that commercial and financial interests were the primary forces that needed to be balanced against the non-elite social classes, in the three branches of government.

Beard showed that the Founding Federalists all had a personal vested financial interest in skewing the results of the new constitutional rules to suit their own needs, while at the same time, attempting to ensure stability in the government by establishing rules of procedure that balanced financial factions against each other.

Stability, used in this historical sense, means perpetual constitutional rules that can never be revoked, even when it becomes obvious that the rules are destructive of the ends that they were intended to achieve.

The end goal, for Madison was financial and economic stability, not liberty.

This is the point, in contemporary time, that citizens find themselves with usurpation of liberty by the Democrat Marxists, in the election of November 3, 2020.

It is obvious that Madison's constitutional rules, in the hands of Democrat Marxists, are destructive of the ends of liberty, stated in the Declaration.

And, like the farmers of the 1880s, Rush listeners and Trump voters, have discovered that they have no method of re-gaining authority from the Marxists.

Madison stated in Federalist 10,

> "The most common and durable sources of factions has been the various and unequal distribution of property…creditors, debtors, landed interests, manufacturing interests mercantile interests, a moneyed interest."

Madison argued that,

> " …the real threats to rights in a republic lay not in arbitrary acts of government misruling its people but in the more disturbing possibility that

popular majorities,(non-elites), acting through government, would willfully trample on the rights of individuals and minorities," (the well born)."

Madison feared that if the non-elite democratic forces at the state level ever achieved unified power over all three branches, at the national level at any one time, the central government would collapse into an undemocratic tyranny.

As Hamilton explained,

> "Every community divides itself into hostile interests of the few and the many, the rich and well-born against the mass of people If either of these interests possessed all the power it would oppress the other…we [the natural aristocracy] need to be rescued from the democracy."

Hamilton's favorite term of endearment for the farmers, and non-elites, was "the howling masses." [deplorables].

Or, as James Dickson stated at the convention in 1787, the new constitution must protect,

> "the worthy [natural aristocracy] against the licentious. [the deplorable farmers]"

Madison shared the opinion of Jonathan Jackson that the main threat of tyranny originated in the excesses of democracy [populism] at the state level.

In his 1788 book, Thoughts Upon The Political Situation in the United States, Jackson wrote,

> "A natural aristocracy that had to dominate public authority in order to prevent America from degenerating into a democratic   licentiousness, into a government where the people would be directed by no rule but their own will and caprice... Tyranny by the people was   the worst kind because it left few   resources to the oppressed (the elites)."

The farmers, in western Pennsylvania, in 1792, had been trying to pay their taxes in paper money, not in gold and silver, as preferred by the elites who owned government bonds.

Less than 5 years after 1787, Hamilton had succeeded in creating an oppressive aristocracy, and Hamilton led an army of 13,000 federal soldiers into western Pennsylvania, in 1792, to crush the farmers who refused to pay their excise taxes in gold and silver.

As do the Democrat Marxists today define society in collectivist terms of oppressed groups, and not comprised of individuals.

Hamilton noted,

> "all parts of society were of a piece,
> that all ranks and degrees were
> organically connected through a great
> chain in such a way that those on top
> were necessarily involved in the
> welfare of those below them."

There was no gold and silver in circulation for the farmers to pay their taxes. And, when the farmers did not pay their taxes in gold and silver, the Federalist tax collectors came and took their farm lands, and gave the lands to the aristocrats, in payment of debt on government bonds.

One hundred years later, when the farmers of 1887 did not repay their debts to the bankers and merchants on a timely basis, the government agents came and took their farm lands.

This later strategy of taking the land away from the farmers, in the 1880s, was called the "debt-lien" system, all perfectly legal under the constitutional rules established by Madison.

According to Hamilton, payment of taxes and debt repayment, by the farmers, in paper money issued by the state governments, was "oppressive."

"Oppressed" in this Federalist usage meant the oppression of the well born by the licentious non-elites, who were using state government to re-write laws on credit and debt payment.

John Dickson explained that Madison's new Federal constitution placed the remedy,

> " in the hands (well born) which feel the disorder of democracy, [populism] whereas the antifederalists placed the remedy in the hands of citizens (the common people), who cause the disorder, by not paying their taxes and debts in gold and silver."

Madison's rules took away the farmer's ability to pay their taxes in paper money, issued by the states.

Madison, in Article 1, Section 10, centralized the power of the federal government on debt repayment, at the state level, by eliminating the power of the states to regulate debt contracts.

The political problem that Madison left America with, beyond precipitating the Civil War, was that his constitutional system eliminated the ability of non-elite classes to reclaim the government from the socialists.

This inability to reclaim fair rules was the same issue faced by the agrarian populists, and the same issue faced by Rush listeners, today.

As Gordon Wood has pointed out, in The Creation of the American Republic, not only did Madison's scheme provide for a system dominated by,

> "...natural leaders who knew better than   the people as a whole what was good for society," but it also succeeded in removing the non-natural leaders from the political process."

Wood noted,

> "In fact, the people did not actually participate in government any more... The American (Federalists) had taken the people out of the government altogether.

The true distinction of the American system, wrote Madison in Federalist #71,

> "lies in the total exclusion of the people, in their collective capacity in any share in the government."

As soon as Madison's constitution was published, George Mason stated on September 15, 1787, that the plan of amendments was exceptionable and dangerous.

He stated,

> "As the proposing of amendments is in both modes to depend in the first immediately and in the second ultimately on Congress, no amendments of the proper kind would ever be obtained by the people, if the Government should become oppressive."

Mason went on to say that Americans had been duly warned about the incipient aristocratic tyranny.

> "These gentlemen who will be elected senators, will fix themselves in the federal town, and become citizens of that town more than of your state. This government will commence in a moderate

aristocracy. It is at present impossible to foresee whether it will, in its operation, produce a monarchy or a corrupt, oppressive aristocracy, it will most probably vitiate some years between the two, and then terminate in the one or the other."

We identify George Mason as one of the first American populists, because he believed, as did Jefferson, that the citizens, themselves, were their own best judges of protecting their financial interests.

Mason had written the Virginia Declaration of Rights, prior to Jefferson's Declaration. The two documents are similar in text, with Jefferson's use of the term "pursuit of happiness," for Masons right of property.

Mason wrote,

"Inherent rights" to which all men are born include the enjoyment of life and liberty, with the means of acquiring and possessing property, and pursuing and obtaining happiness and safety."

We place Rush's natural rights ideology into Mason's American tradition of populism, formally recognized in history as the "anti-federalist" populist tradition.

The intractable political problem Madison left the nation is that when the Republicans abdicated their historic mission of protecting the natural rights of working class citizens, there were no rules identified in Madison's constitution to "alter or abolish" the incipient Marxist tyranny.

Voting for representatives of the uniparty globalist agenda does not represent a legitimate choice for citizens.

However, the way that Madison wrote the election laws for the House and Senate made his two party political arrangement irrevocable.

When Rush more recently describes the collusion of RINO Republicans with Marxist Democrats, he was in the process of giving up that the Republican Party would somehow morph into a credible conservative party.

What Madison overthrew, in 1787, was the voluntary economy of exchange of the Articles of Confederation, where common citizens could freely gain the value of their labor (property).

Madison replaced the Articles, which were based upon equal commercial exchanges, with unfair government rules, where the elites dominated the terms of exchange with their unbalanced, and unchecked government power.

Madison's flaw was his deliberate omission, in the Preamble, that the ultimate goal of the constitution was protecting individual freedoms. This flaw of omitting the end goal results in a dysfunctional government that is commonly described as the "Arrow Paradox," where dysfunctional policies cycle over and over again, in a type of computer do-loop.

To answer Tom Watson's question, obtaining labor's fair share today means creating better constitutional rules for the fair distribution of income, by restoring the moral values of the natural rights republic.

That American belief in fair constitutional rules is called populism.

We place Rush into this American tradition because of his advocacy of fair rules for all citizens, as did the leaders of the agrarian populist revolt.

The way out of this globalist conundrum, for Rush listeners, and Trump voters, is to restore a constitutional version of the Articles of

Confederation in Jefferson's natural rights republic.

The rules of the new constitution are aimed at a fair system of economic exchange, where society is made up of self-made citizens, who are not slaves to the government.

Chapter 6. Fitting Rush's Advocacy of Free Market Capitalism Into the Entrepreneurial Capitalist Economic Growth Model.

Rush's statements about entrepreneurship were generally placed in the context of the supply of investment capital destroyed by wasteful government spending.

His basic philosophy was that the capitalist system provided opportunities for ordinary citizens to achieve prosperity, and that government spending reduced the supply of capital.

> Jun 27, 2007 We're At War for America's Survival.
>
> In short, you can't have capitalism without capital. You can't create new jobs in the private sector unless there's a new or expanding business to create those jobs. And since new and expanding businesses require capital for investment funding, if you tax that capital more, you get less investment and fewer jobs.

Rush focused on the burdensome regulations and the tax code as examples of how the government destroyed the supply of capital, and beginning in

2007, began connecting the problems of Big Government to a malfunction in the American two-party political system.

Rush stated,

> "The impression we all get is that representative republicanism doesn't work. Elected representative republicanism is not working. The frustrating thing about that is, that the Republicans are going on along [with the Democrats] in their own demise. Unbelievably, shockingly, they're going along with it, for whatever reason. It's inexplicable. So how does this all relate to the guy who called from Boston who wanted to buck up? I don't want to be dramatic here, but we really are in a war for the survivability of the kind of country we've always had, and want to have in the future."

Rush's analysis of the potential demise of the American economy in 2007, were echoed by his statements in 2020, about fighting for the survival of the Nation, after the election had been stolen in November of 2020.

We extend his statements about the relationship between economic growth and entrepreneurship, and place them into the theoretical framework of economic growth theory to place his ideology into an entrepreneurial capitalist economic model.

We revisit the earlier statements by James Buchanan about how the rules of the constitution determine the income distribution, or as economists say, "the welfare outcomes," of the economy.

Following Buchanan, we claim that there is only one unique configuration of constitutional rules that leads the economy to the highest point of welfare maximization.

We claim that the causal mechanism that leads the nation to the highest point of welfare maximization is individual entrepreneurship, based upon rules that allow for maximum individual liberty.

Economists describe this theoretical point of maximum welfare with the aid of a diagram that describes Pareto Optimization, where no individual citizen's welfare can be improved, without causing a decline in another citizen's welfare.

This diagram is extremely important to the entire theoretical edifice of neo-classical marginal economics, and tends to fascinate the imaginations of most economists.

They describe the point of Pareto optimality in theological terms of heaven, or as most of them say, "economic nirvana."

It is not our mission to explain the macro economics of why or how this diagram is created by the economists.

Our mission is to use this diagram as the starting point to place Rush's statements into the entrepreneurial capitalist framework.

Diagram 1. Pareto Improvement From Inferior Point of Pareto Inefficiency.

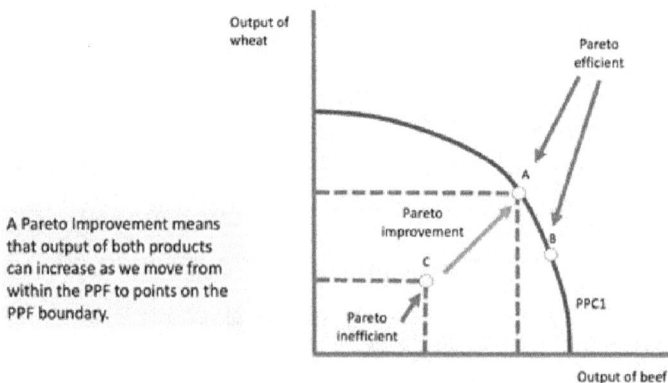

A Pareto Improvement means that output of both products can increase as we move from within the PPF to points on the PPF boundary.

Output of wheat

Pareto efficient

A

Pareto improvement

C

B

PPC1

Pareto inefficient

Output of beef

The interior box that describes the Pareto inefficiency, at point C, is based upon the concept of wasted resources that are not being used in the most efficient manner.

By moving those inefficient resources to a better use, at point A, the entire economy experiences economic growth, visualized in the diagram as an outward movement of the Production Possibilities Frontier.

In Democrat Marxism, it is the Marxist elites in the vanguard party, who make the judgments and decisions on how to move inefficient resources to their more efficient use.

In crony corporate global capitalism, it is the kleptocrat ruling class that determines what resources are used and what is produced, in order to skew the benefits of production to themselves.

In entrepreneurial capitalism, it is the individual entrepreneur who decides how to make money by moving capital resources into a business that the consumer market desires.

We describe the resources in the inefficient box, at point C, in terms of the kleptocracy of the crony global capitalist model of economic growth.

The items in that box include graft, corruption, wasteful government spending, regulations, increased taxes, and lobbying costs in The Swamp.

Our point is that the economy would reach a higher point of production efficiency if those wasted resources were eliminated, and reverted to use as capital, for investments by entrepreneurs.

We have written elsewhere that the welfare outcomes of the entrepreneurial capitalist model provide the most fair outcomes, possible, in terms of income distribution. (Vass, Laurie Thomas, The American Millennial Attraction to Socialism: Comparing the Economies of Chinese Communism, Crony Corporate Capitalism, European Crony Socialism, and the American Free Enterprise Innovation Economy, 2020, GabbyPress.com).

Achieving that optimal social welfare outcome depends on the configuration of the constitutional rules that govern voluntary allegiance of citizens to the rule of law.

We place Rush's advocacy of entrepreneurism into this framework of fair constitutional rules, in order to reclaim the American Dream.

Aug 8, 2013. We Have a Grand Opportunity to Inspire a Country Engulfed in Pessimism

This is a YouGov poll. This is about people's attitudes and the American dream. And the headline of the story is: "More Dems than Republicans, 53% to 27%, say American Dream is Dead." Fifty-three percent of Democrats think the American dream is dead. Twenty-seven percent of Republicans think it's dead. "We are Americans. We can do whatever we want. Whatever obstacles are in our way, we can find our way around them." That's been the history of our country. It's been the history of greatness, the greatness of our nation. I will never forget back in the '90s, white collar people were laid off for the first time in the modern era at greater numbers than blue collar people were. They had to do something. And many of them took the risk of starting their own businesses, becoming their own bosses. I remember the calls that we got in those three days. People had never been happier they said, never felt more satisfied. They may not be earning any money yet, but they were doing what they loved. They enjoyed getting up every day and they felt like they had been reborn.

When economists move from a discussion of Pareto Optimality, in production efficiency, to social welfare, they modify Diagram 1 in order to show the relationship between production and income.

We describe this transition in Diagram 2, which shows the political power of the kleptocracy to determine what products are produced.

The kleptocrat ruling class derives the power to rule the economy from their positions of power in both the Republican and Democrat Marxist political parties, not as a result of transactions in the free competitive market.

In Diagram 2, Point E represents Pareto optimality in the entrepreneurial capitalist economy, as determined by consumer choice.

Point F describes the production under the ruling class kleptocracy, which skews production away from free market choices of consumers to economic outcomes that benefit the kleptocracy.

Diagram 2. Transition From Production Sphere to Income Welfare Sphere. 2-Commodities.

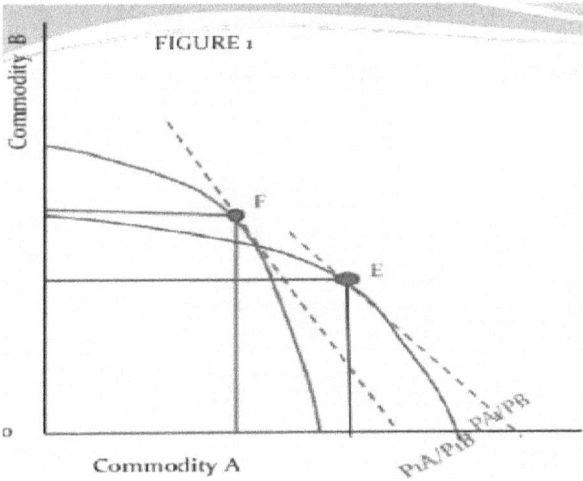

FIGURE 1

Commodity B

Commodity A

F

E

O

P_1A/P_1B

P_A/P_B

As an example, in the military-industrial component of the kleptocracy, the production output features jets and submarines, rather than houses.

From Diagram 2, economists add the idea that social welfare optimality is achieved at the point where all citizens are indifferent between one welfare outcome versus any other welfare outcome.

The indifference curves express the idea of income distribution between social classes.

Diagram 3 describes 3 different levels of social welfare, arranged along a social welfare function, where income is distributed between 2 social classes, the kleptocrat ruling class and non-kleptocrats.

Diagram 3. Social Welfare Function In 2-Social Class Economy: Kleptocrats and Non-Kleptocrats.

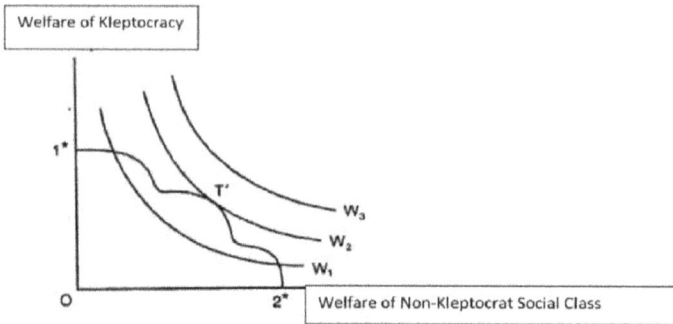

Fig. 15.6 : Social Welfare Function

The political power of the kleptocrats allows them to enforce a suboptimal level of income for non-kleptocrats, W(1), while the kleptocrats enjoy a higher level of unearned income (rent seeking), at the point of tangency r, along income distribution W(2).

In addition to the political power to skew income distribution to themselves, the ruling class also re-shapes the social welfare function closer to the vertical axis because of their prior power to control what products are produced.

The much higher level of social welfare in Diagram 3, at W(3), reflects the welfare outcome of the entrepreneurial capitalist economic growth model.

Rush states his advocacy of entrepreneurism,

> "We are Americans. We can do whatever we want. Whatever obstacles are in our way, we can find our way around them."

We interpret his statement to reflect his desire of maximum social welfare, for all citizens, along an outward expanding social welfare function.

Achieving maximum social welfare is dependent and contingent on the configuration or rules in the constitution.

In the entrepreneurial capitalist model, the interpretation of justice as fair constitutional rules is dramatically different than the Rawlsian/Marxist notion of fairness that relies on a set of elites who judge the fairness of welfare outcomes and have the power to shift income from one social group to another.

The Democrat Marxists start out with the initial assumption that individuals do not have a rational self-interest, and that only the socialist elites can determine what is in the best interests of any individual, who is defined by the socialists as a cog in a collectivist social group (feminists, gays, blacks, poor people, etc.).

That initial starting assumption is also embraced by the ruling class kleptocrats, who collude with the Democrats to make income distribution decisions, after the kleptocrats have made the production output decisions that benefit the kleptocrats.

We argue that Madison's constitution was defective in establishing fair rules of economic exchange because he thought that the natural aristocracy would make better collective decisions than the populist decisions of common citizens.

We revert back to Buchanan to support our argument that there is only one configuration of constitutional fair rules that leads to both maximum production efficiency and maximum social welfare.

Buchanan begins by placing his theory of constitutional economics into the natural law foundation of Locke by describing the scientifically natural functioning of the human brain to seek welfare optimization.

His first principle of the logic of natural law is that all individuals are rational in the pursuit of their own sovereign life mission,

In The Theory of Public Choice, (1972), he defines an individual not so much from the perspective of insight-imagination, but from the brain's rational choice attribute.

He states that,

> "…we can simply define a person in terms of his set of preferences, his utility function. This function defines or describes a set of possible

trade-offs among alternatives for potential choice."

In The Reason of Rules. (2000), Buchanan explains the importance of how citizens provide prior consent to follow the rules that they give to themselves.

"Just conduct," writes Buchanan, "consists of behavior that does not violate rules to which one has given prior consent."

In other words, rather than relying on the separation of powers to deal with the problem of the class conflict between elites and common citizens, as Madison did, Buchanan relies upon the natural law rationality of self-interest as a force that binds individuals to society as a process of human rationally to optimize welfare, in decision making environments.

In leaving the state of nature, and forming a constitution, Buchanan explains, that individuals are placed in a position of uncertainty in the outcome of their life's mission.

In setting rules, no individual knows in advance where the individual may end up, given the choice between one set of constitutional rules or another.

His logic of individual rationality is that any individual, with a rational self-interest, would choose fair rules for all, aimed at the greatest freedom for all.

Buchanan wrote,

> "To the extent that Madison's constitution commands little respect, it is, in part, because it fails in its function of limiting the scope of both governmental and private intrusion into what are widely held to be protected spheres."

In The Reason of Rules, Buchanan and Brennan write,

> "Our specific claim is that justice takes its meaning from the rules for the social order within which notions of justice are to be applied. To appeal to considerations of justice is to appeal to relevant rules. These rules provide the framework within which patterns of distributional end states emerge from the interaction of persons who play various complex functional roles."

In other words, fair distribution of income and wealth, under Buchanan, is obtained through just rules of financial and economic exchange, that are defined in the constitutional contract.

Buchanan reasoned that constitutional rules were required to reduce the chance situation that a citizen would be subjected to the arbitrary police power of the state.

He wrote,

> "Uncertainty about just where one's own   interest will lie in a sequence of plays or rounds will lead a rational person, from his own interest, to prefer rules and arrangements, or constitutions that will seem fair, no matter what final positions he might occupy."

Buchanan argues that the issue of economic fairness must be determined through the process of making and enforcing fair constitutional rules, not on manipulating welfare outcomes, as enforced by the Rawlsian/Democrat Marxists.

Buchanan explained that every set of constitutional rules has an internal end-goal to which the rules are directed. The end goal, or telos, of the natural rights constitution, given the initial natural law assumption of rational self-interest, is individual freedom.

In Logical Foundations of Constitutional Liberty, (1999), Buchanan relies on a philosophy of logic to explain how the end goals of a constitution, clearly stated in the preamble, create the binding allegiance of citizens to follow the rule of law.

One set of constitutional rules promotes the national sovereign economic interest.

The other side promotes corporate globalism, which directs economic benefits to global banks and corporations.

Buchanan argued that there is only one, unique, configuration of constitutional rules that leads the nation to optimum rates of national economic growth. These rules aim at maximum individual freedom to allow individuals to seek their own happiness.

We claim that Buchanan' philosophy of maximum individual freedom is consistent with Rush's natural rights ideology.

When Rush states that Americans can do anything, he is channeling the principles of liberty in Jefferson's Declaration.

The linkage from Jefferson to Rush's advocacy of the entrepreneurial economy is through the mechanism of private capital investment in entrepreneurial ventures that causes future economic growth.

The relationship between constitutional individual freedom and national economic growth is through the ability of individuals to invest private capital into new technology ventures that commercialize new technology products.

The new technology products create new future markets that create new flows of income.

In the entrepreneurial model, technical change causes new income flows to be created where none had existed before.

Part of the new income is a result of increased productivity, meaning that output increases with reduced inputs in the production unit.

Part of the new income is in the form of profits related to new goods produced by new production units.

Another part of the increased income is in the form of wages and salaries paid to people who work in the new units, who spend their incomes in the local economy, creating income and employment multipliers.

National economic growth is a contingent outcome of the type of technical change, in the economy. It occurs in some nations, but not in others, because of the rules of economic freedom in the constitutional contract.

Rush believed that the greatest freedom and independence for citizens is offered by the operation of the free and competitive market.

We extend Rush's belief in entrepreneurial capitalism to incorporate Buchanan's fair constitutional rules that allow entrepreneurs to pursue their prosperity and happiness by creating new ventures and owning their own businesses.

As a consequence of property rights in the entrepreneurial economy, the entrepreneur appropriates the value of her production, not the crony corporation or the state.

The entrepreneurial economy promotes tacit knowledge creation and is characterized by unique cultural values associated with individual risk taking and creating new ventures.

The entrepreneur provides an ingredient to the process of technical change that is absent in the framework of the crony capitalist corporate economy.

The entire process of economic growth caused by open flows of knowledge can be seen as the shifting of the national production function outward, which is reflected by changing technical coefficients in a dynamic input-output model the national economy.

Brink Lindsey, of the Niskanen Center, (2017), aptly summarizes what has become a widespread consensus among scholars from many different fields within the economics profession:

Lindsey writes,

> "The long-term future of economic growth hinges ultimately on innovation. Indeed, as Sachs and McArthur have stated, "The more we think about it, the more we realize that technological innovation is almost certainly the key driver of long-term economic growth."

We claim that Rush's natural rights ideology fits into the entrepreneurial capitalist growth economic model.

Chapter 7. The Counter-Attack on the Marxist Democrat Smear of Rush's Natural Rights Conservatism.

In the weeks after Rush died, Marxist pundits and talking heads, began a public relations smear campaign to place Rush's natural rights conservatism into their class war and race-based interpretation of the American founding.

The Democrat Marxists have an endearing psychological trait that projects onto their enemies the psychological defects and deficiencies that possess the Marxists.

We argue that the nature and intent of the Marxists can be determined by simply examining what they are projecting onto their enemies.

In their smear of Rush, they allege that he has no coherent ideology of liberty. Turning this projection on its head, the Marxists have no coherent definition of liberty because liberty is not the end goal of their ideology.

They project onto Rush, the race-based white supremacist argument that Rush's philosophy is based on white grievance, in the antonym of their own Black grievance of slavery, beginning in 1619.

The intent of the Marxists is to revise the history of Rush in order to transform his natural rights conservatism into the left's social construction of reality that Rush was a white supremacist.

Marxism denies the absolute truth of Locke's natural law because the left's ideology does not accommodate western empirical scientific logic.

Natural law claims there is a natural order to the universe, specifically to human existence, that can be discerned by human reason.

The absolute natural law language of the Declaration leaves no doubt as to the truths upon which the nation was founded, a truth that the Marxist deny.

The moral relativism of global socialism, and its logical cousin, "Critical Legal Studies," cannot exist in the same reality with self-evident truths. One, or the other, logical philosophy, must be vanquished from the historical public record.

In their totalitarian quest to destroy any philosophy that opposes their vision, it is imperative for Marxists to destroy the historical reality of Rush's natural rights conservatism.

Their smear of Rush is intended to vanquish, from the historical record, any trace of Rush's natural rights conservatism.

If they are successful in their smear, there would only be one version of the historical truth about Rush's 31 years of broadcasting, the Marxist version of history.

Our intent is to document Rush's natural rights conservatism, in order to counter the historical lies of the Marxists about Rush.

Our interpretation of natural rights conservatism is based upon the relationship between Jefferson, and 84 years later, Lincoln, as the new interpretation of modern American conservatism.

We view both Jefferson and Lincoln as the modern incarnation of American conservatism, and we trace this synthesis between them to the analysis provided by Harry Jaffa's path breaking book, The Crisis of the House Divided (1959).

Jaffa described how Lincoln was faithful to the Declaration in his justification of the Civil War because Lincoln believed that the natural law and natural rights expressed by Jefferson in the Declaration provided moral justification for the Civil War.

We cite James Pierson, in his 2020 article, Conservatism is Rooted in Natural Rights, in The American Conservative.

Pierson writes,

> "The emergence of a more distinctively American version of conservatism is based upon the Founding Fathers, the nation's founding documents, the writings and speeches of Abraham Lincoln— and, of course, [Locke's] natural rights philosophy limiting government to a few important duties."

After Jaffa's modern conservative synthesis of Jefferson and Lincoln, Ronald Hamowy, described Jefferson as "Mr. Natural Rights."

Hamowy writes,

> "It is beyond dispute that Jefferson embraced the conclusions about the nature and functions of government put forward by John Locke a century earlier. Not only did he regard Locke as one of three greatest men who ever lived... following Locke, Jefferson argues that once government violates our

rights we are at liberty to take any actions we deem appropriate to put a halt to these violations, including the overthrow and replacement of the civil authority."

Writing about Jefferson's Declaration, James R. Stoner, Jr., described the links between Locke's natural law and Jefferson's concept of liberty.

Stoner writes,

"Americans generally did not see a practical distinction between natural law and the common law, nor between natural rights and British liberties... Political liberty is the right of men to rule themselves... political liberty and natural law went together: Nature summons man, individually and collectively, to self-government and guides him in the exercise of his power of choice. The exercise of political liberty leads men to make their own laws and so in that respect can obscure its natural law foundation."

We agree with Stoner that the Nation's fundamental basis of natural law has been obscured in recent American history because the

Republican Party did not champion the cause of liberty.

We place Rush into the new American tradition of natural rights conservatism as a champion of natural law and natural rights in the founding of America, and begin our counter-attack on Democrat Marxists from this point.

In contrast to western empiricism that discovers truth through scientific observation, the truth of a proposition for Marxists is in the degree and intensity of allegiance shown to the proposition by its adherents.

For example, the more the Marxist Democrats declared that Trump was a racist, the more intense their allegiance to their truth that Trump was a racist.

In each of our examples of the Marxist smear below, we rely on the Marxist social construction of reality to explain how and why the Marxists smear the natural rights legacy of Rush.

Bill Scher, a Marxist writer for Washington Monthly, provides an example of the left's projection psychology by using both the left's use of "grievance", as if it was Rush who had grievance, and the left's use of class war hatred as the force that binds Rush listeners to natural rights ideology.

Scher writes,

> "The broadcaster traded in bigotry and humor, homophobia and entertainment– for the purpose of building a conservative movement. But like Trump, he could only harness grievance. Even with his extraordinary clout, Limbaugh couldn't forge a belief system, a positive vision. He could only harness grievance."

Bob Moser, writing in Rolling Stone, turns the left's disbelief in western logic onto Rush, as if it was Rush who disbelieved in scientific empiricism, and as if it was Rush who was spreading hatred.

Like Scher, Moser invokes the Marxist propaganda of victimhood of Rush's listeners

Moser writes,

> "[Rush] spread hate, racism, and lies, and laid the groundwork for Trumpism... sources matter as little as facts or logic. What makes sense in [Rush's} parallel universe is whatever distracts and absolves white, non-liberal Americans

from blame, guilt, or responsibility. It's whatever reminds them of both their supremacy and their victimhood. It's whatever emboldens them to strike back at the evil left-wing empire that is always busy plotting to subjugate them and destroy America As We Knew It."

The projection of Moser's social construction of reality is that it is conservatives who are plotting to subjugate other citizens, and destroy "our democracy," not Democrat Marxists, who overthrew the American government in their successful coup in November, 2020.

The intent of Moser is to denigrate Rush's natural rights conservatism as if Rush did not have a coherent political philosophy.

Moser writes,

"But try — even today — naming one policy that Rush Limbaugh famously pushed, or one conservative idea he advanced. What the self-proclaimed "instrument of mass instruction" really advanced, from the get-go, was a purely Manichean view of politics: Our side all good, their side all evil… The Pandora's box of right-wing nuttery that Limbaugh brought into the mainstream will be loose on the land for the foreseeable future. There's no putting the lid back on it now."

Conor Friedersdorf, writing in the Atlantic, emphasizes "the aggrievement of Rush," in projecting onto Rush, Friedersdorf's own grievances against America.

"[Rush wanted to] to avenge a deeply felt sense of aggrievement. Limbaugh and Trump were alike in attaining great wealth and political influence while still talking and seeming to feel as though society was stacked against guys like them… Limbaugh advanced the smug hatred of liberals and feminists, took pleasure in mocking the left, fueled the ugliest impulses of his audience more often than he sought to elevate national discourse, boosted Republican politicians (whatever their policy preferences) until the end, and died an identitarian populist who betrayed the philosophy he long extolled."

Friedersdorf's intent is to describe Rush's ideology as race-based class hatred, projecting onto Rush the race-based class hatred of Democrat Marxists for conservatives.

Whatever else Rush may have been, he was not an advocate of race-based identity politics, when he died.

In an earlier 2016 article in the Atlantic, Friedersdorf makes the claim that Rush did not have a coherent, or consistent ideology of natural rights conservatism, because of his endorsement of the non-conservative Trump.

Friedersdorf writes,

> "Limbaugh has abandoned conservatism as his lodestar. All else being equal, he still prefers the ideology. But it's now negotiable. He'd rather have a non-conservative nominee [Trump] who attacks and is loathed by the Republican establishment than a conservative who is conciliatory and appealing to moderates. And Trump was uniquely suited to bring him to this point."

Friedersdorf very helpfully identifies Jeb Bush as representing the type of "true" conservative, most preferred by Marxists.

Friedersdorf writes,

> "Jeb Bush now portrays his struggling campaign for the Republican nomination as a vehicle for defending conservatism. "I do think it's important that the conservative party nominate a conservative, and someone that understands the role of America in the world [globalism]," Jeb said. "What I want to do is make sure that the conservative cause is advanced. Not just in talk shows and think-tanks and wherever conservatism is talked about in all sorts of different ways, but in governing."

In his Mother Jones article, How Rush Limbaugh Taught Me How to Think Like a Piece of Shit, Jacob Rosenberg emphasizes the left-wing narrative that Rush did not have a coherent philosophy.

Rosenberg writes,

> "For me, that was Rush's power. He
> presented conservative dogma as what
> it is: pure reaction. Did he have a core
> belief system itself? No. Of course not...
> for so many the appeal of bullshit like
> Limbaugh's and Trump's is that
> creates an air of freedom of a certain
> kind—no need for consistency, no
> values to uphold, no kindnesses required.
> It is permission—big pause here—to be
> an asshole."

Writing in Politico, John Harris goes for a twofer
by citing the left's aggrievement narrative and the
no-coherent ideology narrative about Rush.

> "For 25 of the past 30 years, no
> public figure more fully represented
> the aggrieved soul of the American
> Right than Rush Limbaugh...Rush
> stated "There cannot be a peaceful
> coexistence of two completely
> different theories of life, theories of
> government, theories of how we
> manage our affairs. We can't be
> in this dire a conflict without

something giving somewhere along the way." ... Limbaugh and Trump represented a psychological movement more than an ideological one. It is unified by shared dislikes — of the media, of civil rights activists, of know-it-all professors, of feminists, of preening, hypocritical liberal politicians, of anyone who, they perceive, assumes a pose of moral superiority toward the cultural attitudes and lifestyle of traditional middle Americans."

In an almost perfect rendition of the left's psychological projection onto their enemies, Harris makes the point that it is the conservatives who promote hate, and that it is conscrvatives who have a morally arrogant philosophy to impose their totalitarian views on non-conservatives.

In all of their projection of hate, and in all of their sleazy assertions that Rush was a racist, the Marxists never cite Locke, Jefferson, Thomas Burke, George Mason, or Lincoln to make their case that Rush did not have a coherent ideology of liberty.

The reason for this omission of the citation to ideological authority is that the Marxist authority of their stunted ideology is Marx.

At its bare essence, Marxian philosophy embraces the first principle of legal positivism that there are no absolute truths.

The Marxist Democrats believe that there is no absolute moral right or wrong. There is only the truth of their ideology that capitalism leads to racism, upon which America was founded.

In their worldview, only the Marxists are capable of passing laws aimed at correcting the moral sin of slavery.

If the Marxist pundits were ever to admit the authenticity of the lineage of Rush's natural rights conservatism, they would be forced to counter his tradition of Jefferson and Lincoln, with their intellectually vacuous ideology of Marx, and the vapid legal positivist writings of Cass Sunstein.

Chapter 8. What To Do After the Panic Subsides That America Has Died.

Rush could never tell his listeners that it was time to panic because he could never bring himself to admit that the Marxist Democrats won the war, in their coup of November 3, 2020..

Part of our mission in placing Rush's ideology into the American tradition of natural rights conservatism is to extend his ideology into a strategy of what his listeners, and the 75 million Trump voters, do next.

Our mission is to place our interpretation of Rush's natural law/natural rights philosophy into the constitutional framework of a democratic republic, whose end goal is the defense of liberty in an entrepreneurial capitalist economy.

We advise Rush listeners to embrace the reality that America has died, and that it is time to move on to a nation whose end goal is liberty.

We believe it is silly for Rush listeners, and Trump voters, to continue to believe that the Former United States (FUSA) can be rehabilitated.

We believe it is silly to believe that the MAGA Humpty Dumpty can be put back together again, up on the wall.

It is senseless to attempt to launch a Trump conservative movement within the establishment Republican Party.

We advocate that a better idea is to deploy the new American conservatism of Rush to create a new nation, whose constitution aims at correcting Madison's flaws of FUSA.

Madison created a social class-based constitution that attempted to check and balance financial conflict between the natural aristocracy, and common citizens.

Madison's idea ended on November 3, 2020, in a centralized Marxist tyranny, with an unelected puppet that imposes Marxism on the majority of citizens, against their will, and without their consent.

A better constitution would replace Madison's class conflict model with Buchanan's fair rules that promoted voluntary allegiance to the rule of law.

As Buchanan points out, voluntary allegiance to the rule of law results from the realization that it is in one's best interest for his or her life's mission to be consistent with the public purpose of liberty for all.

We believe this philosophy of the voluntary allegiance to the rule of law captures the essence of Rush Limbaugh's natural rights conservative political philosophy

From around 2007, Rush had been expressing doubts and uncertainty about the functioning of the American representative republic. In particular, he expressed his concern that the establishment Republican Party was not acting like a conservative party.

Rush could not tell his listeners that it was time to panic because he hoped that one day, in the future, that the Republicans would become the party of conservatism.

We explained elsewhere that Trump had a small window of opportunity to re-mold the Republican Party, before he was removed from office. (Vass, Laurie Thomas, Trump's 4 Year Window of Opportunity to Replace the Crony Capitalist Republican Party With a Conservative National Sovereignty Party. The Citizens Liberty Party News Network, www.clpnewsnetwork.com.

That opportunity was lost, along with the principles of Madison's representative republic, in the Marxist Democrat coup of November 2020.

We agree with Thomas West, in his 1988, Heritage Foundation article, Conservatives, Liberals, and the Founding: The Meaning of the Debate Over Natural Rights.

West writes,

> [Madison's constitution] served well enough in its time; but now it is time to junk it and get on with something   else. That "something else," of course, may turn out to be less attractive, once it is stripped of its pretended continuity   with the past. It may well mean the legitimizing of centralized government by unelected "experts" controlling every detail of our lives from birth to death."

We agree that the new constitution will not be based upon the "pretended continuity" with Madison's flawed document.

The new constitution is based upon the natural rights conservatism of Jefferson and Lincoln, and changes Madison's centralized representative republic with a decentralized state sovereignty framework, in a democratic republic.

The new constitution replaces Madison's nominal nothing of a Preamble, with the following preamble of the principles of liberty.

Preamble to the new constitution of the Democratic Republic of America:

We, the citizens of the Democratic Republic of America, establish this constitutional contract between our respective states and the National Government of the Democratic Republic of America.

We solemnly swear and affirm that we establish this contract to preserve and protect the natural and civil rights of citizens in each state, and to protect and defend the sovereignty of each state and the nation, from foreign and domestic threats.

By freely and voluntarily joining our state government into the union of Democratic Republic of America, we affirm that the National Government will be guided by the following principles:

"…that all legitimate government authority is derived from the consent of the citizens governed…"

"…that those governed by the laws and whose individual freedom is restricted by the laws should have the greatest say and consent in making of the laws…"

"…that those who make the laws and give consent to the laws, acting as representatives of the citizens, bind themselves and their constituents to following the laws..."

"...that individual citizens who freely give their consent to form a government through constitutional conventions are bound by the original contract until the operation of the government becomes destructive to the original intent of obtaining individual freedom and the pursuit of happiness..."

"...that the parties to the constitutional contract are individual citizens acting through their elected representatives at the state and national levels of government..."

"...that the citizens of each state have mechanisms in place in the constitutional contract to modify or abolish the national government, including the right of each state to vote on remaining a member of the national government in a referendum to be held every 20 years from the date of admittance..."

"...that as the consequence of the sovereign authority of citizens, citizens have an inalienable natural right to remove an elected representative from office upon a referendum of 51% of registered voters in a state..."

"...that the National Government is instituted to allow individual citizens to pursue individual happiness and to limit the arbitrary application of government power over the lives of individuals..."

"...that the National Government that is created by this union of states shall never usurp the sovereign power or authority of the individual states or the sovereignty of the citizens in each state and that states have an inalienable right to call a convention of the states, without Congressional approval, to modify, amend, or abolish this Constitutional Contract."

"...that an individual's private property obtained through legal contract and title transfer, their rights to appropriate income and profits from the use of their private property, and their rights to dispose and transfer their private property are inviolate and derived from natural rights granted to them by God, and that no government or constitutional contract may ever abrogate or subordinate these natural individual rights..."

"...that a citizens Grand Jury of 18 citizens is impaneled, for a term of 12 months, to protect and preserve the rights of citizens against the arbitrary application of government power against citizens..."

"...that a citizens Grand Jury of 18 citizens must inspect all national penal facilities within its district every 6 months, and report their findings to the Chief District Judge, who shall act to remedy the deficiencies found by the Grand Jury…"

"…that the 1776 American Revolution was ordained by God to allow citizens to pursue individual human freedoms and liberty from oppression and is an exceptional model in human history…"

"…that all citizens are created by God with equal natural rights, and that the purpose of the Nation is to protect the equal application of the law to all citizens, regardless of race or religious beliefs…"

Citizen Bill of Rights of the Democratic Republic of America.

We affirm and swear that all citizens in each of the respective states of the Democratic Republic of America are guaranteed equal rights for all, and special privileges for none. Among them are:

1.   That all citizens are due the equal application of justice and that no citizen is entitled to special or unequal treatment of the application of the law.

2.   That all citizens have a natural right to worship and exercise their own religion and that the National Government is prohibited from making and enforcing any law respecting the

establishment of an official national religion and compelling citizens to worship a national religion.

3.   That all citizens have a natural right to truthful and honest statements from government agents and from elected representatives, and that it is the duty of the free press to report the truth.

4.   That the most certain form of protecting civil liberties is guaranteeing that all citizens in the respective states have a natural right to own and use weapons, and a right to organize themselves into citizens militias, and that the National Government shall make no laws which abridge the right of law-abiding citizens from owning, keeping and bearing weapons to defend themselves from tyranny.

5.   That citizens have a civil right of action against elected representatives or agents of the National Government, for violation of the natural rights of citizens, upon a presentation of a motion of grievance to a Grand Jury of 18 citizens, who shall hear the case and determine the outcome and set the penalties for the violation by a majority vote.

6.   No citizen in any state shall be seized or imprisoned, or stripped of his rights or possessions, or outlawed or exiled, or deprived of his standing in any other way, nor shall agents of the government proceed with force against him,

or send others to do so, except by the lawful judgment of a true bill of indictment by a majority vote of a grand jury of 18 citizens, or by the rules of judicial civil procedure of the National Government.

7. The National Government shall be prohibited from making or enforcing any law that restricts the natural right of a citizen's freedom of speech and freedom of conscience.

8. The National Government and any state or local government is prohibited from making or enforcing any law which restricts the right of citizens to peaceably assemble, and to petition the National Government for a redress of grievances.

9. The National Government is prohibited from using agents of government or national resources to conduct searches and seizures of private citizen documents, and that the documents obtained from illegal searches and seizures are inadmissible in any national court.

10. The National Government, and every State government, are prohibited from making or enforcing any law which shall abridge the privileges or immunities of citizens of the Democratic Republic of America; nor shall any State deprive any person of life, liberty, or property, without due process of law; nor deny to

any person within its jurisdiction the equal protection of the laws.

11.   No citizen shall be deprived of life, liberty, or property, without due process of law; nor shall private property be taken for public use, without just compensation, determined by a majority vote of a Grand Jury of 18 citizens.

12.   That all citizens are judged innocent until proven guilty in a trial of due process.

13.   No warrants or judicial orders in any criminal investigation shall be issued by a national court, except upon probable cause, determined in a judicial hearing, supported by an oath or affirmation of the government agent describing the specific items or locations to be searched and a judicial description of the crime being investigated.

14.   No person shall be held to answer for a capital, or otherwise infamous crime, unless on a presentment or indictment of a majority vote of a Grand Jury of 18 citizens who conduct an inquiry into the legitimacy of the government's allegation of a national crime.

15.   No citizen shall be subject for the same offence to be twice put in jeopardy of life or limb; nor shall be compelled in any criminal case to be a witness against himself.

16. In all criminal prosecutions, the accused shall enjoy the right to a speedy and public trial, by an impartial jury of the State and district wherein the crime shall have been committed, which district shall have been previously ascertained by law, and to be informed of the nature and cause of the accusation; to be confronted with the witnesses against him; to have compulsory process for obtaining witnesses in his favor, and to have the assistance of counsel for his defense.

17. The right of trial by jury shall be preserved, and no fact tried by a jury, shall be otherwise re-examined in any Court of the Democratic Republic of America, than according to the rules of the common law then obtaining in the national judiciary.

18. Excessive bail shall not be required, nor excessive fines imposed, nor cruel and unusual punishments inflicted, nor imprisonment for longer than 5 days, in the absence of specific charges and allegation of crime.

19. The Citizens Grand Jury in any State retains the right of initiating a citizen initiative on legislative proposals by a petition to the House of Representatives, which must respond to the petition within 30 days of receipt.

20.   The right of citizens of the Democratic Republic of America America to vote, hold elected office, or deliberate in public debates, shall not be denied or abridged by the National Government or by any State on account of race, color of skin, sex, or religious beliefs.
......

The entire institutional edifice of voluntary compliance to the rule of law is built on the principles stated in the Preamble of the Natural Rights Constitution of the Democratic Republic of America.

In closing we reaffirm our agreement with Rush that we are Americans.

We can do anything.

We have created a new nation before.

We have fought for liberty throughout our history.

We will fight again for liberty and equal justice for all.

We are Americans. We can do anything.

About Laurie Thomas Vass.

Laurie Thomas Vass is a North Carolina constitutional economist.

Vass is a graduate of the University of North Carolina at Chapel Hill and has an undergraduate degree in Political Science and a Masters degree in Regional Planning.

She was a professional money manager with her own investment advisory firm for 30 years, and was cited by Peter Tanous, in The Wealth Equation, as one of the top 100 private managers in the nation.

She is the inventor and holder of a research method patent on selecting technology stocks for investment accounts.

Vass is the author of 12 books, and over 130 scholarly economic articles on the Social Science Research Network author platform. She is currently ranked in the top 1.1% of over 550,000 economic authors, worldwide, on the SSRN platform.

Her articles on the SSRN platform are available for free. She is a student of North Carolina history and public policy, and her books and articles about the state are archived in the Carolina Collection, at Wilson Library, UNC.

www.ingramcontent.com/pod-product-compliance
Lightning Source LLC
Chambersburg PA
CBHW050737030426
42336CB00012B/1611